F.A. FOMAN

SELF HYPNOSIS

The Ultimate Guide on Using the Power of Hypnosis
For You and Your Business, Learn How You Can Use
Hypnosis to Get Your Mind to Make Money for You

Descrierea CIP a Bibliotecii Naţionale a României
F.A. FOMAN
  SELF HYPNOSIS. The Ultimate Guide on Using the Power of Hypnosis For You and Your Business, Learn How You Can Use Hypnosis to Get Your Mind to Make Money for You / F.A. Foman – Bucharest: Editura My Ebook, 2021
  ISBN

F.A. FOMAN

SELF HYPNOSIS

The Ultimate Guide on Using the Power of Hypnosis For You and Your Business, Learn How You Can Use Hypnosis to Get Your Mind to Make Money for You

My Ebook Publishing House
Bucharest, 2021

TABLE OF CONTENTS

Foreword

Hypnotherapy is a capital instrument for relaxation and alleviating stress. It helps calm down both the mind and body, giving a useful „respite". All the same it can be rather costly to hire a clinical hypnotherapist, and we might not always want one around when we would like to de-stress. This isn't a problem, as it's possible to do self hypnosis, and this book will show you how to achieve self hypnosis as well as the benefits to you and your business.

Self hypnosis is the greatest method known to men to bypass the interference and resistance of the aware mind and implant instructions directly into the Subconscious mind.

CHAPTER 1

LET'S GET STARTED-RELAXING

Synopsis

We will have a look at the first step to achieving self hypnosis.

Relaxation

In the first place, you'll need to make certain that you will not be distracted for at the least half an hour, preferably an 60 minutes. Switch off phones, and tell loved ones and friends not to trouble you. Find a comfy place. Someplace that's neat and tidy, and of a comfortable temperature.

Reduce the lighting if this assists you. If you like, you could fire up some candles and burn some incense. You are able to be seated, or you can lay down – whichever you favor.

Importantly make certain that your legs are not crossed, as they could end up going to sleep after half an hour.

1. Shut your eyes and conduct ten easy deep breaths – in by the nose, and out by the mouth. Say to yourself the word „Relax' on every out breath.

2. Conceive of yourself at the top of ten steps, with a doorway at the bottom. With every slow step you take downward, feel yourself getting more deeply relaxed.

3. Once you arrive at the bottom open the door to your paragon place of relaxation. It may be a beach, a garden, anyplace. It could be someplace real, or imaginary – your own uniquely particular relaxing haven.

4. Utilize as many senses as you are able to. Take a good look about. Pause and hear all of the sounds. Maybe you are able to hear the call of a bird, or the wind gently blowing out. Perhaps you are able to smell the angelic scent of flowers, or the salt in the ocean? Touch things, and make the experience as actual as you potentially can.

5. Explore your unstraining haven, and enjoy it for as long as you want.

This is a bang-up strategy to help relaxation, and your ability to loosen up will improve the more you do this. Most of us don't relax anywhere near enough, and this can harm our health and our businesses in many ways.

Lack of relaxation can break down our immune systems, making us become more prone to malady. Poor relaxation may as well increase temper, anxiety, poor attention span and sadness. These troubles can affect our behavior, increasing our likelihood to overeat, smoke, drink, takes drugs etc. Even if you just do this relaxation work, you'll massively improve your total health and business in almost every area.

CHAPTER 2

WHAT THE TRANCE IS ABOUT

Synopsis

Unless you have previously been in a hypnotic state you may not know what it is about.

The Trance

If you're struggling with the technique of self hypnosis and becoming completely relaxed, then hang in there. Moving into a hypnotic state is a skill that will get better over time.

Don't anticipate too much, hypnosis isn't the "magic state" that the mass medium frequently portrays it as being. You'll in all likelihood still be cognizant of what is going on around you, and might well think "is this it?" All the same you'll notice the difference when you awake.

It might be worthwhile visiting a clinical hypnotherapist, or purchasing a recording at least one time, in order to get the feeling of a trance. When you have felt a trance a couple of times, you'll be more informed as to what frame of mind you're seeking.

You'll have experienced a hypnotic trance a lot of times in your life. It's the frame of mind where you're so absorbed in a book or movie that you become lost in that domain. It's that frame of mind where you drive for miles without thinking, and you don't understand how you managed to get to your destination. It's that frame of mind where you gaze into space, daydreaming about nothing in particular.

To deepen the trance or hypnotic state you will direct your mind to go into a deeper and deeper state of hypnosis by counting gradually from ten (10) to zero (0). Some individuals prefer to count upwards from 1 to 20. Here is what you will tell yourself:

As you count slowly from 10 to zero, tell yourself that you are relaxing deeper at each and every falling number.

To heighten the hypnotic state even more, duplicate this countdown one or more times.

As well us this technique if you like:

Mentally focus your attention on different parts of your body and mentally require those parts to loosen up, with no exertion, withoutforcing:

Begin by telling your feet to relax by directing your attention to your feet and restating several times mentally and absent of force. "Relax both feet, relax both feet." Some individuals get better results by mentally restating "My feet are relaxing". Some even use the second person „You" as in "John, your feet are relaxing" or even "John, relax both feet". Restate this instruction several times as you feel your feet starting to relax. Don't try to make your feet relax. Just permit them to relax.

CHAPTER 3

HOW TO PUT SELF HYPNOSIS TO WORK

Synopsis

Just what do you do once you are truly relaxed?

Making Hypnosis Work For You

You are able to as well take this self hypnosis a bit further if you want. You are able to learn to give yourself specific therapy as you become more established. Here are a few strategies you are able to use after you have reached relaxation.

What the mind conceives of, it trusts has really happened. If you conceive of something bad happening to you, you'll feel the emotions as though it's truly happening. This can make the mind distressed, as it will inwardly trust that these things have truly happened to you.

Success spawns success, so if you envision yourself achieving something, then it will help you to do simply that. You might wish to envision yourself slimmer, healthier, more successful or wealthier forinstance.

Or you might wish to envision yourself having achieved something, like a promotion or a new job. Make the image as real as you are able to, use as many of your senses as you are able to, and do this as frequently.

You're only limited by your vision. As a matter of fact you should notice that your creative mightiness increases the more that you use self hypnosis, as your mind gets more accustomed to using its creativepowers. Stick with it.

What I sometimes discover is that individuals will stop using hypnosis once they've made the essential improvements that they wished to make. All the same this may finally deny you the overall benefits of the increased relaxation, as affairs may slowly slip back to where they started. Set a particular time to do it, even if it's only onceor twice a week, and stick to it. If you have particular subjects that you wish to deal with, then step this up accordingly, perhaps daily fora few weeks.

This technique will help some of you to better your mental and physical well-being, and realize what a safe and powerful tool for change hypnosis is. As many people as possible should live long,healthy and happy and successful lives.

CHAPTER 4

PROGRAMMING FOR MONEY

Synopsis

Now is the time to put self hypnosis to work to help your mind make you money.

Turn Your Brain Into A Money Machine

Now that you are deeply relaxed, it is time to embed (= program) into your Subconscious a few useful statements to help you accomplish your goals. You may supply any instructions of your own design.

You will merely restate each instruction about twenty-thirty times. There is no need to be worried about a rigid count. The more relaxed and untroubled you are when you repeat your instruction, the more inforce they will be.

At this time, do not waste your time attempting to envision anythingor feel some deep feeling.

Simply take the plan of attack of being the boss who is giving some directions to his servant. There is no need to scream, no need to force.

The less agitated you can feel at the time of giving these directions,the faster they will produce the end-results you want.

Good example: (For the financial area) The succeeding are the instructions you will give to yourself, one at a time, and restating eachone about twenty-thirty times (or more if you wish to) prior to going to the following instruction and without making any efforts whatever.

Simply think about these instructions sinking deeper and deeper intoyour subconscious mind:

1. I am a money attracter.

2. I draw in money like a magnet.

3. I pull in money quickly and easily.

4. I am a millionaire. (apply "Every day I am becoming more and more financially well-fixed" if you have a hard time accepting "I am amillionaire").

Observe: You may as well use different arrangements such as "John,you are a money magnet", or even "John, BE a money magnet".

Try out different things and find out which format is most well-situated and natural for you.

CHAPTER 5

SELF CONFIDENCE THROUGH HYPNOSIS

Synopsis

The only way to truly succeed in this life and your businessis to have ample self confidence.

Boost Your Self Image

Are you as confident as you would really like to be? Numerous individuals discover that they are subdued from reaching their full potentiality due to a deficiency of self-confidence. The fundamental thing about self-confidence is that it is all in your mind – it is about how you believe and what memories, opinions and thought habits you have shaped since you were young. That which stems from your ideas, conscious and subconscious can be easily changed using your mind.

But it is not as simple as just making up one's mind that you want to think otherwise, and boost your self-confidence. A really important part of taking on new beliefs and change is to make them into automatic habits.

Making them things that you do automatically without having to consciously think about them. As human beings, we are by nature resistive to change. It takes the average person a minimum of twenty- one, conscious repetitions of a new conduct, before they replace an old habit with a new one. So reading this self-help book once is not enough.

There is an easy and efficient way of altering habits and building new subconscious programs. You can use self-hypnosis and guided visualization to get at and re-program your subconscious mind in order to give rise to permanent change in the shortest possible time.

Professionally designed self-hypnosis or plans enable you to access thought patterns, mental attitudes and beliefs that you may not even be consciously cognizant off and replace them with new ones. They also direct you to do active inner searches to enable you to get at undeveloped resources that you can use to help you achieve your potentiality.

A well designed self-hypnosis program will maneuver you through a conscious and subconscious process of releasing negative programming of failure and defeat that you have assembled from childhood on. They motivate you to seriously evaluate all the reasonswhich you think have added to your lack of confidence, and then to substitute unconscious programming that is no longer of benefit to you.

A well put together self-hypnosis program can outfit you with a powerful guided visualization that you can do whenever you experience your confidence going down, which will fill you with the foregone conclusion that you are capable of achieving the task aboutwhich you were doubtful.

CHAPTER 6

GOAL SETTING WITH HYPNOSIS

Synopsis

Having goals is one thing...attaining them is yet another.

Learn Better Ways To Achieve Your Goals

One highly powerful benefit of using hypnosis is the power to train your mind to stay centered on the successful accomplishment of your goal. You will be able to program a specific effect and retain the ability to consciously divert your attention to it in a favorable, success-affirming manner. You can as well eradicate self-sabotage and remove the negative feelings and ideas that are blocking your path to success.

Here are a few ideas for using hypnosis as a goal accomplishmenttool.

1. **Envision**. Program yourself with your desired result. While under the influence of self hypnosis visually imagine that your goal is already achieved and your objective has been accomplished. See it as true. See it through your own eyes and feel all the marvellous feelings associated with that goal accomplishment.

2. **Doggedness**. Get down into your subconscious mind and alter your inner character traits to match those people who never quit. Program your subconscious mind to be relentless regardless of what is going on in any given state of affairs. Post hypnotic suggestions to formulate an iron will and relentless approach to your goals will be priceless in times of stress and disenchantment.

3. **Believe Positively**. Discover how to think positively. The subconscious mind has a disposition to replay past memories and cast them back into consciousness in the form of questions and fears. Through the practice of self hypnosis you are able to completely eliminate them. Program your subconscious mind to believe positively and anticipate positive results.

4. **Program out the Trouble.** Inevitably some trouble will arise when you go after worthwhile goals. Through hypnosis you are able to solvethese troubles reasonably quickly. While in trance see yourself successfully passing over the obstacle. You don't have to see how you did it, just visualize yourself at the other side, alleviated, happy and proud that you "figured it out" and reached the other side. If this, in itself, is a problem for you, or you find it difficult to do then look for the advice of a qualified hypnotherapist. A competent hypnotherapistwill determine the root of your trouble probably in the fits consultation!

5. **Pre-pave your route.** Conceive of yourself meeting the correct people and being in the correct place at the correct time. Program your mind like this, by the power of hypnosis, and your subconscious mind will pick up on non-verbal hints, process the 1000000s of bits of information you receive every minute and guide you to the right course of action.

6. **Develop Trust.** utilise hypnosis to convince the subconscious mind that your destination is already a reality. "Fake it till you make it". Fool your subconscious mind into thinking the "real" world is really exactly like the world you

26

have been envisioning. In the profoundly relaxed state that hypnosis offers you are able to get fully involved in your mental image. Truly feel how great it is to have already achieved all those things you wanted for so long. Enjoy the fact that you're enjoying the benefits of having accomplished that goal.

CHAPTER 7

STRESS MANAGEMENT

Synopsis

You must manage stress to keep your life and your business.

Kill The Stress

One who's working online, there are times that a virtual assistant would be so strained out. I've been working now for a long time now in this industry and a lot of times that I have put up with stress.

A lot of people would think that working online is all amusing. Yes, there are rewards than working the usual office jobs but not all the times. There are also cases that you'll feel like stepping down. There are more misdirection's at home than in the office. Some family members don't comprehend that you're working and deadlines, goalsand targets need to be met.

For one who's many projects, trouble arises on time management. One truly finds it difficult to achieve several projects in a day. Social media sites could sometimes take away the absorption of an online worker. Also the change in the matters or markets that you're workingon also makes it hard to finish particularly if you're not so familiar about the subjects.

For the common office workers, there are also several stressors whichmay include: working long hours, getting stuck in traffic or long traveltime, rival at work, huge workloads, money troubles, family troubles, huge debts, charge plate bills, etc.

Stress can evidence through insomnia, indigestion, hypertension, anxiety, headaches, depression, ulcers, chest ache, drug addiction oralcohol addiction.

There are drugs that could relieve these troubles but those are just impermanent. One may be relieved in a short-term but in the long- term, he/she might be addicted to the drugs or the drug may not evenwork. Also, these drugs can take a vast part of your budget which can add up to one's fiscal problem. Drugs are just blocking out what you feel but don't take away or solve the root cause of the trouble.

A cheap way to alleviate stress is self hypnosis. Self hypnosis doesn't need great sum of money in order to practice. The moment you've learned how to practice, it's enough!

Self hypnosis is a mighty tool that anybody can benefit from. But naturally one needs to believe in it first in order to make it work. One shouldn't doubt its effectualness. Practice of self hypnosis may pave way for tackling concerns related to stress management.

This practice can alter the programming of one's subconscious mind. When the mind achieves a relaxed state, we can de-emphasize ourselves and rejuvenate our minds leading to a renewed feeling.

A stress-free feeling can then lead to productiveness.

CHAPTER 8

HOW CAN HYPNOSIS HELP YOU

Synopsis

There are tools for you top ramp up your business and hypnosis is one?

What Can It Do For Me

Maybe you felt guilty about creating money? Maybe you felt that ifyou bring in more money then somebody else will lose out?

We all accept mental blocks which prevent us from achieving any more success and riches than we believe we're capable of achieving. For example, just think for a minute about how much income you would like to earn in the next year. Now, whatsoever figure you came up with is a block in itself. Why didn't you think of a more eminent figure?

If you did not say 'I prefer to become a millionaire', then ask yourself how come.

Many individuals have become millionaires only to lose it all and then bring in a fortune all over once again. It's in fact a comparatively common example of lightning striking twice. Making income is truly no different from any other destination. Making money doesn't necessarily mean cheating others or even compromising your own values. Many good and honored inhabit in the world whose sincerity can never be doubted have, even so, made a fortune along the way.

Mental blocks and constraining self-beliefs stop us from accomplishing all that we're capable of accomplishing as a human race. If you don't trust in spite of appearance that you'll earn enough revenue to free yourself from worry and difficulty and to enjoy life more, then you won't. If you begin to believe in the possibility then the chances are you'll start to change your behavior and thought actions appropriately.

Hypnotherapy can begin to help you to believe in yourself, to arm self confidence and motivation and to acquire well defined consequences for your life.

Hypnosis won't make you steal, lie or cheat, as a matter of fact it can't 'make' you do anything at all. It can all the same help you to expand your beliefs and understanding of money and how to make more of it.

Hypnosis is about authorization and imagination, and can assist youto empathize your own massive value.

Conceive of yourself in the future tense having discovered your true value. Conceive of clearly that you've earned a fortune and you're expecting to increase your fortune. Ask yourself a couple of questions;

What did you have to do to get at that place?

What impressions did you have to change about yourself or the worldin order to earn your destiny?

Exactly how much more income do you prefer to make? What are you going to do with his knowledge?

We commend starting your journey by working at these and othercrucial questions. You'll then find plenty of other valuable advice, resources and links on the net.

CHAPTER 9

IS IT SAFE?

Synopsis

You want to try it but you wonder if it's safe.

Self Hypnosis Is Safe

Self hypnosis is a arena of interest that is not only circled by numerous myths, but a lot of individuals also have the incorrect thought of what it is and what it may do. Even a accidental remark of this matter to the casual mortal can get a response that shows how little the issue is known and translated.

Many individuals in reality consider it to be charming and even the mass media has portrayed it in and of itself. All the same, appropriately used, self hypnosis can assist a individual in complete growth in their own lives, and it can as well assist in raising the self.

As a matter of fact, self hypnosis has as well been used as a means of rehabilitation in many medical infirmaries and facilities all over the world and with many acquirements also. Just in case if you need adjustment and want to step-up your physical and mental welfare you need to toy with using self hypnosis as a means of actualising these dreams.

Even tho' self hypnosis has been applied by numerous individuals that have found it to be helpful, there are a number of congenital dangers to it also that needs to be translated and avoided. It's therefore crucial to take precautions before attempting self hypnosis so that the chance of any mishap are eliminated or diminished.

Self hypnosis can be rather complicated and it does, at the very lowest, mean placing the self under a trance like setting to advance relaxation and enter the subconscious mind. After you come through in hypnotizing, your subconscious will be aroused and any suggestions you say to it will be recognized in a more clear way thereby ensuring that your mind responds in the wanted behavior.

The only concern with self hypnosis is that it can become dangerous under particular states of affairs such as when you meander outdoors while still hypnotized and do matters that can hurt you. In addition, you may do things inadvertently that may put your life in danger.

Truth be told, you'll become vulnerable when performing self hypnosis and to forestall risking your well-being you should guarantee that you do things in a style that guarantees your well-being.

A way of insuring that self hypnosis works for you without periling your life is to take recourse to using a self hypnosis CD which is commonly readily accessible on the market today.

Differently, you are able to steer clear of trying self hypnosis and opt instead for better methods of achieving personal well-being including getting a certified hypnotist to hypnotize you or you are able to even entertain using brainwave enhancement to help you complete your ambitions.

CHAPTER 10

COMING OUT

Synopsis

Returning to an awake state.

Coming To

When you've completed your self hypnosis sitting you'll begin up the stairs counting backwards from the tenth stair. As you climb the stairs tell yourself you are coming up from hypnosis and will awake with a feeling of wellness. Once you have made your way up the staircase then tell yourself to open your eyes and return to the normal awake state.

At this time, you're ready to break through when it comes to your trance state. You'll achieve this by telling to yourself mentally thefollowing:

"It's now time for me to open my eyes and get alert again. At the count of 5 I'll open my eyes, I'll be wide awake, feeling refreshed, re- energized, reclaimed, rejuvenated and ready to go . . . 1 . . . 2 . . . 3 . . .ready to open my eyes . . . 4 . . . 5 . . . (snap your fingers) . . . eyes open, unsleeping, wide awake and ready to go. This is the end of this hypnotic session".

That's all you have to do. Very simple. No complex visual image, no complicated NLP routines. The simpler, the better and more effectualyour hypnotic session will be.

You may understand by now that this tool being taught to you heremay be used to bring you the hoped results in ANY area of your life.

5. WARNING

• Keep your hypnotic session to no more than 20 minutes.

• Practice at any rate twice EVERY single day. The more you practice, the deeper and faster you'll go into the hypnotic (trance) state and thebetter your instructions will become.

• Use a maximum of FIVE instructions per sessions.

Wrapping Up

We all have mental blocks which prevent us from achieving any more success and wealth than we believe we are capable of achieving. For instance, just think for a moment about how much money you would like to earn in the next year. Now, whatever figure you came up with represents a block in itself. Why didn't you think of a higher figure?

Self hypnosis can do your body ... your mind... your body... and your business good. Explore your options!

9 787693 494095

Printed by Libri Plureos GmbH in Hamburg, Germany